1

HILLARY CLINTON

THE UNSTOPPABLE FORCE

A Biography of the Woman Who Shattered Glass Ceilings and
Paved the Way for a New Generation of Leaders

George Humphrey

TABLE OF CONTENTS

A Synopsis of Hillary Clinton's Life Story

On October 26, 1947, Hillary Diane Rodham Clinton was born in Chicago, Illinois. Her childhood home was in the Chicago neighborhood of Park Ridge, Illinois. Her mother, Dorothy Howell Rodham, was a stay-at-home mom, while her father, Hugh Rodham, had a modest company.

After attending Wellesley College, Clinton earned an honors degree in 1969. She enrolled at Yale Law School after that, earning her degree in 1973. Following graduation from law school, Clinton worked for the Little Rock, Arkansas-based Rose Law Firm as a lawyer and as an advocate for children.

Bill Clinton, the attorney general of Arkansas at the time, and Clinton were married in 1975. In 1979, Bill Clinton was elected governor of

Arkansas, and from 1983 until 1992, Hillary Clinton presided as the state's first lady. As the First Lady of Arkansas, Clinton focused on health care and education reform. She was also a part of the Whitewater scandal, which included a real estate transaction in which Hillary and Bill Clinton were involved.

Bill Clinton won the US presidential election in 1992. From 1993 until 2001, Hillary Clinton held the position of First Lady of the United States. Clinton worked on several projects as First Lady, one of which was the Children's Health Insurance Program (CHIP). She supported women's and children's rights and participated in international diplomacy.

Clinton won a seat in the US Senate from New York in 2000. From 2001 until 2009, she was a senator for California. Clinton addressed a wide range of topics as a senator, such as the environment, healthcare, and international affairs.

President Barack Obama named Hillary to be the US Secretary of State in 2009. 2009–2013 was her tenure as Secretary of State. Clinton worked on a range of international policy problems as Secretary of State, including the intervention in Libya and the Arab Spring.

Clinton entered the 2016 presidential election. Although she was the Democratic Party's nominee for president, Donald Trump defeated her in the general election.

Her Global Influence

The globe has been significantly impacted by Hillary Clinton. She has campaigned to advance democracy and human rights throughout the world and has been a prominent advocate for the rights of women and children. She has also been a vocal supporter of taking action against climate change and environmental conservation.

Clinton's role as the US First Lady contributed

to her rise to prominence internationally. Among the many projects she worked on was the Children's Health Insurance Program (CHIP), which has given millions of American children access to health insurance. She supported women's and children's rights and participated in international diplomacy.

Clinton continued to work on a range of international policy topics while serving as Secretary of State. She was a fervent supporter of the Libyan intervention and the Arab Spring. She also made efforts to advance human rights and democracy globally.

Why Is Hillary Clinton Important to You?

One of the most significant political personalities of our day is Hillary Clinton. Her entire life has been devoted to improving the public good and the state of the globe. She serves as an inspiration to girls and women everywhere.

Clinton's tale demonstrates fortitude and tenacity as well. She has triumphed over several obstacles in her life, like as the Lewinsky incident, the Whitewater dispute, and her defeat by Donald Trump in the 2016 presidential contest. Clinton has persisted in trying to improve the world despite these obstacles.

We should all take inspiration from Hillary Clinton. She demonstrates to us that despite our challenges, we are capable of realizing our ambitions. She also instills in us the value of compassion, tenacity, and persistence.

In Park Ridge, Illinois, growing up

On October 26, 1947, Hillary Rodham was born in Chicago, Illinois. Her childhood home was in the Chicago neighborhood of Park Ridge, Illinois. Her mother, Dorothy Howell Rodham, was a stay-at-home mom, while her father, Hugh Rodham, had a modest company.

Clinton had a contented and encouraging upbringing. She participated in the debate team, Girl Scouts, and student government, among other things. She excelled academically as well, earning accolades for her high school diploma.

Yale Law School and Wellesley College

Clinton enrolled in the esteemed women's college in Massachusetts, Wellesley College, in 1965. Her major was political science, and in

1969 she received an honors diploma.

Clinton participated in several extracurricular activities at Wellesley, including the Young Republicans Club, the debate team, and student government. In addition, she belonged to the Children's Theatre Group at Wellesley College.

Following his graduation from Wellesley, Clinton went to Yale Law. There were just 29 women in her class of 104. Clinton participated in several organizations at Yale, including the Yale Political Union and the Yale Law Journal. She also assisted renowned legal researcher Professor Charles Reich in his studies.

Clinton received honors from Yale Law School in 1973. She was among the first female Yale Law School graduates, having graduated first in her class.

Her Earlier Legal and Advocacy Career

Clinton relocated to Little Rock, Arkansas, to work for the Rose Law Firm upon his graduation from Yale Law School. She rose to the top of the firm's legal ranks rather rapidly.

Bill Clinton, the attorney general of Arkansas at the time, and Clinton were married in 1975. In 1979, Bill Clinton was elected governor of Arkansas, and from 1983 until 1992, Hillary Clinton presided as the state's first lady.

Clinton worked on several issues as the First Lady of Arkansas, including healthcare and education reform. She was also a part of the Whitewater scandal, which included a real estate transaction in which Hillary and Bill Clinton were involved.

Bill Clinton won the US presidential election in 1992. From 1993 until 2001, Hillary Clinton held the position of First Lady of the United States.

Clinton was ready for a career in public service

because of her upbringing and education. She was an intelligent and driven student who participated in several extracurricular activities that helped her gain expertise in public speaking and leadership. Her early work as an advocate and lawyer also equipped her with the knowledge and expertise required for success in the public eye.

Clinton's tale serves as motivation for all of us. She gives us hope that regardless of our upbringing, we can realize our aspirations. She also instills in us the value of perseverance, hard effort, and commitment.

Bill Clinton's marriage and relocation to Arkansas

Hillary Rodham wed Bill Clinton, the Attorney General of Arkansas, in 1975. In 1979, Bill Clinton was elected governor of Arkansas, and from 1983 until 1992, Hillary Clinton presided as the state's first lady.

When Hillary Clinton married Bill Clinton and relocated to Arkansas, she was hesitant to give up her legal profession. Nevertheless, her spouse finally persuaded her to go to Arkansas with him.

After arriving in Arkansas, Hillary Clinton plunged headfirst into the public eye. She worked on several problems, such as healthcare and education reform. She contributed to her husband's political career as well.

Her Reforms in Healthcare and Education

Hillary Clinton worked on several causes as the First Lady of Arkansas, including healthcare and education reform. She was a fervent supporter of raising the standard of public education and early childhood education. She also made an effort to increase healthcare access for all Arkansans.

Clinton established the non-profit Arkansas Advocates for Children and Families in 1983 to enhance the quality of life for children and families in Arkansas. Additionally, she was a member of the board of directors of the Children's Defense Fund, a nationwide children's advocacy group.

Arkansas was greatly impacted by Clinton's efforts to overhaul healthcare and education systems. She contributed to raising the standard of education in the state and

14

increasing everyone's access to healthcare in Arkansas.

Her Part in the Whitewater Debate

Bill and Hillary Clinton were involved in a real estate transaction in the 1980s that led to the Whitewater scandal. The Whitewater Development Corporation was a property development project in which the Clintons invested. The Clintons lost money, though, as the project fell through.

The Whitewater Independent Counsel conducted a protracted inquiry into the Whitewater scandal. Although the probe revealed no proof of the Clintons' misconduct, it did harm their reputations.

For Hillary Clinton, the Whitewater affair was a trying moment. Both the public and the media kept a close eye on her. She did, however, continue to work on healthcare and education reform and to assist her husband.

One of the pivotal moments in Clinton's career was her involvement in the Whitewater scandal. It demonstrated her fortitude and dedication to public service.

Clinton had a fruitful and prosperous tenure as Arkansas's first lady. She had a great influence on the state and worked on many key topics. She grew stronger and more resilient as a result of the lessons she gained from the Whitewater incident.

Among her first ladyship initiatives s the Children's Health Insurance Program (CHIP).

Throughout her tenure as First Lady of the United States (1993–2001), Hillary Clinton worked on several projects, one of which was the Children's Health Insurance Program (CHIP). Millions of low-income children are covered by the federal CHIP health insurance program.

Clinton was a fervent supporter of CHIP and was instrumental in its approval in 1997. Millions of children now have access to high-quality healthcare because of the enormous success of CHIP.

As First Lady, Clinton worked on several other projects in addition to

CHIP, such as:

* Education reform: Clinton was a fervent supporter of raising the standard of public education and early childhood education. She also made efforts to increase college access.

** Reforming healthcare: Clinton pushed to increase every American's access to healthcare. She also made an effort to lower expenses and raise the standard of healthcare.

* Women's rights: Hillary Clinton was a fervent supporter of these rights. She made efforts to reduce violence against women and advance gender equality.

** Children's rights: Clinton fought tenaciously for these rights. She fought to shield kids from abuse and violence and to enhance their health and well-being.

The United States was significantly impacted by Clinton's efforts as First Lady. She left a lasting impact on the nation and helped millions of Americans live better lives.

The Effect of the Lewinsky Scandal on Her Marriage

The House of Representatives impeached Bill Clinton in 1998 due to his perjury and obstruction of justice during the Lewinsky crisis. The controversy concerned Bill Clinton's extramarital affair with Monica Lewinsky, a White House intern.

The Lewinsky incident caused great pain to Hillary Clinton. She supported her husband but made it plain that she disapproved of his actions as well. The issue profoundly affected Hillary Clinton's personal life and marriage.

Her Position as an International Champion for Women and Children

Hillary Clinton met women and children from all walks of life during her extensive global travels as First Lady. She committed her life to defending the rights of women and children

19

because she was profoundly affected by the injustices that they encounter globally.

Clinton fought to eradicate violence against women and advance gender equality. She also made an effort to shield kids from abuse and violence and to enhance their health and well-being.

Clinton has made a tremendous contribution to the world by advocating for women and children on a worldwide scale. She has had a lasting impact on the globe and helped millions of women and children enjoy better lives.

During her tenure as the First Lady of the United States, Hillary Clinton achieved great success and productivity. She had a great influence on the nation and worked on many key problems. Additionally, incredible credible fortitude and bravery in the face of the Lewinsky affair.

2000 saw her election to the Senate

Hillary Clinton campaigned from New York for the US Senate in 2000. She became the first woman to represent New York in the Senate after winning the race by a slim margin.

One of Clinton's greatest achievements as a senator was her election. It demonstrated her popularity and respectability even in a state that had supported her husband in the presidential election in 1996.

Contributions to the Senate Armed Services Committee

Clinton was a member of the Senate Armed Services Committee while she was a senator. She strove to better the lives of servicemen and their families and was a fervent supporter of the armed forces.

Clinton also made efforts to advance

international security and peace. She was a fervent advocate for the UN and NATO. She also contributed to the fight against terrorism and the containment of WMDs.

Her Advocacy for the War in Iraq

Clinton cast a vote in favor of authorizing the use of force in Iraq in 2002. She thought that Saddam Hussein posed a threat to both the world and the United States and that the latter had to intervene to drive him from office.

But it turned out that going to war in Iraq was an expensive miscalculation. Since then, Clinton has expressed sorrow for her vote to approve the war. She has also stated that the Iraq War taught her a good lesson and that going forward, she would be more hesitant to endorse military action.

Clinton had a successful tenure as a senator. She had a great influence on the nation and worked on many key problems. She gained experience and became a more reflective politician as a result of her blunders, which she also learned from.

President Obama appointed her in 2009.

Hillary Clinton was named US Secretary of State by President Barack Obama in 2009. Obama thought that Clinton was the greatest candidate for the position despite her reputation as a contentious option due to her background and abilities.

Clinton made a significant comeback when she was appointed Secretary of State. It demonstrated that she remained a significant and prominent player in American politics. It also demonstrated President Obama's faith in her skills.

Her Diplomatic and Foreign Policy Work

While serving as Secretary of State, Clinton

tackled a range of international policy concerns, such as:

* The Middle East: Clinton made efforts to advance stability and peace there. She was a fervent advocate of the Israeli-Palestinian conflict's two-state resolution. She also made efforts to stop terrorism in the area.
* Asia: Clinton strove to improve relations between the US and its allies there. She also made an effort to advance regional development and economic progress.
* Europe: Clinton strove to improve relations between the US and its European allies. She also made efforts to advance human rights and democracy in the area.

Clinton was an accomplished and successful diplomat. She succeeded in forging connections with international leaders and promoting US interests everywhere.

Her Contribution to the Libyan Intervention and the Arab Spring

The Arab Spring was a wave of pro-democracy protests that shook the Arab world in 2011. Clinton actively supported the Arab Spring and strove to advance human rights and democracy in the area.

In 2011, Clinton participated in the operation in Libya as well. NATO oversaw the Libyan intervention, a military operation aimed at defending civilians against attacks by Muammar Gaddafi's forces. Clinton conceded that it was a tough choice, but she still backed the intervention.

Although Gaddafi was successfully overthrown by the Libyan intervention, chaos and instability followed. Clinton has stated that she would be more hesitant to support military action in the future as a result of the lessons she learned during the Libyan operation.

Clinton accomplished a lot during his tenure as secretary of state. She had a tremendous effect on the globe while working on several foreign policy problems. In her capacity as Secretary of State, she also showed exceptional talent and diplomacy.

Her Choice to Enter the Presidential Race

Hillary Clinton declared her intention to run for president of the United States in 2015. For many years, Clinton had been preparing for a presidential bid and was considered the favorite to win the Democratic nomination.

Clinton was inspired to run for president by several things. She thought she was qualified for the position of president and had the necessary expertise. She also thought that for the US to meet the difficulties of the twenty-first century, it required a strong and capable leader.

Her Main Opposition Campaign to Bernie Sanders

Senator Bernie Sanders posed a serious threat

to Clinton during the Democratic primaries. Sanders campaigned on a platform of progressive social and economic reforms; he identified as a democratic socialist.

Sanders and Clinton have somewhat different ideas about where the Democratic Party should go in the future. Sanders stood for the progressive element of the party, while Clinton represented the establishment wing.

The Democratic nomination went to Clinton in the end, but Sanders' effort had a big influence on the party. Sanders inspired a new generation of progressive activists and contributed to the Democratic Party's leftward turn.

Her Campaign Against Donald Trump in the General Election

Clinton competed against Republican contender Donald Trump in the 2016 election. Trump was a divisive personality who ran on a populist platform of anti-immigration and economic nationalism.

The future of the US was seen quite differently by Clinton and Trump. Trump stood for a drastic shift from the current quo, while Clinton represented it.

One of the most contentious presidential elections in American history was held in 2016. Trump won the Electoral College and went on to become President, although Clinton prevailed in the popular vote by almost 3 million votes.

Both Clinton and her supporters were deeply disappointed by Trump's victory. Clinton has continued to support progressive causes and be involved in public life, nonetheless.

Her Influence on American Society and Politics

One of the most significant and powerful political personalities in American history is Hillary Clinton. She has held the positions of United States Senator, Secretary of State, and First Lady of the United States. She has also been a strong supporter of global health and development, women's rights, and children's rights.

Clinton has had a significant influence on American politics and culture. She has paved the path for more women to occupy positions of power and assisted in the dismantling of barriers based on gender. She has also supported progressive issues including gun control, healthcare reform, and education reform.

Clinton is a global role model for girls and

women. She demonstrates that, despite hurdles, everything is achievable if you put your mind to it.

Her Position as an Inspiration for Women and Girls

Globally, Hillary Clinton serves as an inspiration for girls and women. She demonstrates that, despite hurdles, everything is achievable if you put your mind to it.

Throughout her career, Clinton has dismantled barriers based on gender. She was the first female representative of New York in the US Senate and the first woman to graduate from Yale Law School at the top of her class. In addition, she was the first female presidential nominee nominated by a major political party.

Clinton is a global source of inspiration for girls and women. She demonstrates to them that regardless of gender, it is possible to fulfill one's aspirations.

Her Ongoing Global Issues Work

Despite leaving public service, Hillary Clinton still working on international issues. She is the creator of the non-profit Clinton Foundation, which aims to advance development and global health.

Millions of lives worldwide have been significantly impacted by the Clinton Foundation. The Foundation has made efforts to lessen poverty, advance education, and provide access to healthcare.

Clinton is a devoted global justice and equality activist. She is an advocate for the underprivileged and a voice for the voiceless.

Though she is a complicated and divisive person, Hillary Clinton has undoubtedly had a significant influence on American politics and culture. Even though she is no longer in public service, she still works on global issues and is an inspiration to women and girls everywhere.

Though her legacy is still being shaped, Clinton has already established herself as one of the most significant and influential politicians in American history.

Timeline of Hillary Clinton's Life and Career

* 1947: Born Hillary Diane Rodham in Chicago, Illinois
* 1965-1969: Attends Wellesley College, graduating with honors
* 1969-1973: Attends Yale Law School, graduating at the top of her class
* 1975: Marries Bill Clinton
* 1979-1981: First Lady of Arkansas
* 1983-1992: First Lady of Arkansas (again)
* 1993-2001: First Lady of the United States
* 2000: Elected to the United States Senate from New York
* 2009-2013: United States Secretary of State
* 2016: Democratic nominee for President of the United States
* 2017-Present: Founder and Chair of the Clinton Foundation

List of Hillary Clinton's Awards and Honors

* 1994: Grammy Award for Best Spoken Word Album for Children for "It Takes a Village"
* 1997: Presidential Medal of Freedom
* 2003: Glamour Woman of the Year Award
* 2009: Time magazine's 100 Most Influential People in the World
* 2013: Fortune magazine's Most Powerful Women in Business list
* 2014: Benjamin Franklin Medal for Distinguished Public Service
* 2016: John F. Kennedy Profile in Courage Award
* 2017: Hillary Rodham Clinton Award for Advancing Women's Health and Human Rights
* 2018: Hillary Rodham Clinton Children's Award for Excellence in Global Leadership
* 2019: Nelson Mandela Award for Leadership from the Elders
* 2020: American Academy of Arts and Letters Gold Medal in Public Service

* 2021: Presidential Medal of Freedom

Hillary Clinton is a highly accomplished and respected figure in American politics and society. Her life and career are an inspiration to women and girls all over the world.

Printed in Great Britain
by Amazon

34898327R00030